HERITAGE TRACTION IN COLO

Volume 4
THE CLASS 40s

Nostalgia Road Publications

The **Heritage Traction** Series™

is produced under licence by

Nostalgia Road Publications Ltd.
Units 5-8, Chancel Place, Shap Road Industrial Estate,
Kendal, Cumbria, LA9 6NZ
Tel.+44(0)1539 738832 - Fax: +44(0)1539 730075

designed and published by
Trans-Pennine Publishing Ltd.
PO Box 10, Appleby-in-Westmorland, Cumbria, CA16 6FA
Tel.+44(0)17683 51053 Fax.+44(0)017683 53558
e-mail:admin@transpenninepublishing.co.uk

and printed by
Kent Valley Colour Printers Ltd.
Kendal, Cumbria +44(0)1539 741344

© Text: Trans-Pennine Publishing Ltd. 2005
© Photographs:Strathwood Collection or as credited

Front Cover: *In August 1968, D206 is seen at Kilmarnock wearing the earliest version of the Inter-City blue livery which was applied to the class from 1967 onwards.* Arthur Wilson (D1401)

Rear Cover Top: *In their early days, The Class 40 Preservation Society promoted their cause on board a condemned 40142 during Crewe Works Open Day in June 1981.* Steve Ireland Collection (D1402)

Rear Cover Bottom: *Heading an MGR coal train from Peckfield to Blythe Power Station, we see 40195 in command of the loading on 17th March 1977, at a time when both the locomotive and our photographer were based at Healey Mills TMD.* Nick Gledhill (D1403)

Title Page: *Part of the later batch of locomotives, D382 is seen just three months into its service life as it approaches Carlisle's Citadel station on 11th June 1962. Allocated to Camden (1B) it is 293 miles into a 401-mile run journey with the Midday Scot from Euston to Glasgow.* Richard Icke (D1405)

This Page: *As if to encourage us to have a look on board, 40188 waits in Llandudno station at the head of the 09.00 departure for York on 17th June 1978. As the image shows, the engine is still very smart following a recent visit to the works.* Colin Whitbread (D1404)

INTRODUCTION

In Volume Two of this series it was shown that the BR-Sulzer Type 4 Peaks traced their development from the immediate post-war London Midland & Scottish Railway and Southern Railway designs of 1Co-Co1 locomotives. The same situation applied with the 'pilot' order of ten English Electric Type 4 1Co-Co1 locomotives, which would become D200 to D209.

There was, however, other experience on which to base the development as from 1948 onwards, the Vulcan Foundry at Newton-Le-Willows (in co-operation with the English Electric Company Limited) had been building generally similar 1Co-Co1 and Co-Co locomotives for the railways of Egypt and Queensland.

Above: *We begin our look at the officially named Class 40s with D210* Empress of Britain, *the first of the Class to be named on 12th May 1960 in a ceremony at Euston Station. Its namesake, the third vessel of that name, was a fine product of the Fairfield Shipbuilding & Engineering Company Limited at their Govan yard. Ordered by the Canadian Pacific Steam Ship Company, it was launched by HM Queen Elizabeth II in 1955 before undertaking its maiden voyage from Liverpool to Montréal on 20th April 1956. The locomotive continued to carry the nameplates until they were removed around 1971, before it was renumbered 40010 under TOPS in 1973. It was withdrawn in 1981 and scrapping was carried out at the Swindon Works of British Rail Engineering Ltd. (BREL), as seen here on 2nd April 1983 when it was seen together with a Peak whilst component recovery was taking place.*
Steve Ireland Collection (D1406)

Below: *Here D211 still carries its* Mauritania *plates when found on what was left of Crewe North shed on 5th March 1967. This Type 4 entered traffic on 23rd May 1959 and was named at Liverpool Riverside station on 20th September 1960. It was re-numbered 400011 in 1973, withdrawn in 1980 and scrapped at BREL Swindon Works. The RMS* Mauritania *was built by Cammell Laird & Co. Ltd. of Birkenhead and launched in 1938, but it was used as a troop ship between 1939 and 1946. A major refit in 1957 made it one of the most luxurious liners of its day, especially after being fitted with air conditioning. It was scrapped at the Inverkeithing yard of Thomas W. Ward & Company Limited, who also finished off 40173 (D373) in 1985. After the demolition of Crewe North shed buildings and the removal of much of the track layout, engines were stabled between duties on sidings with just crude stops fashioned from old sleepers.* Frank Hornby (D184)

Coincidentally on 17th March 1955, in the same year as the BR Modernisation Plan, the Vulcan Foundry (together with its associated company Robert Stephenson & Hawthorns in Darlington) became part of the English Electric Group. In addition to the production of electric and diesel-electric locomotives, Vulcan expanded and started the production of diesel engines suitable for rail traction, marine and industrial applications.

Aside from confirming the last orders for the British Railways (BR) steam fleet with the Standard designs, the British Transport Commission (BTC) committee were charged with the responsibility and the investment funds to modernise our railways. They therefore adopted a number of 'modern traction' designs in various power classifications and placed an initial order for 174 diesel locomotives with different suppliers.

These various designs were to be tested for three years before the results would dictate where the main orders would be placed. Logic suggests that if a couple of years were allowed for the production and delivery of the locomotives, then three years given for evaluation, followed by a further year for the committee to consider its findings, and finally another year at least to commence serious construction, would take it to 1963 before large numbers of the selected locomotives would be available for service.

However, the politicians of the day were committed to removing steam from the railways of Britain at any cost, and as such a gamble was taken with the reliability and suitability of many designs well before 1963.

Above: *Running into Guide Bridge on a balmy summer's day on 24th August 1983 we find 40012 (formerly D212 Aureol) on a train of GUVs. Allocated (as can be seen) to Carlisle Kingmoor Depot (KD), it had started its career at Willesden (1A) on 30th May 1959. It was transferred to Upperby (12B) shed by the time of its naming ceremony on 20th September 1960, and became a regular work-horse around Carlisle. It was named at Liverpool Riverside station (closed in 1971) to celebrate the Elder Dempster Lines ship MV Aureol, which was built by Alexander Stephen and Sons Limited at Govan on the Clyde and launched in 1951. The ship's curved bow, tripod mast and cruiser spoon stern made it one of the most attractive vessels of the day. It was also the largest passenger ship built for the line. Steve Ireland Collection (D1407)*

Below: *Day-trip traffic to locations such as Blackpool, Llandudno and here at Scarborough were always good places to find a Class 40 in the 1970s and the early 1980s. Having a day out on the Yorkshire coast during 1980 is 40013, which carries a painted version of its name* Andania. *A full three years after entering service, EE Type 4 D213 adopted the name* Andania *at Crewe Works in June 1962. It was named after the second ship to be called* Andania *by the Cunard Steamship Company, which had been launched in 1921 by R & W. Hawthorn Leslie & Co. Limited, Hebburn, Newcastle. After entering service, it became a regular on the trans-Atlantic runs to New York, Québec and Montréal, but upon the outset of World War II it was converted to an Armed Merchant Cruiser in 1940. However its service in this guise was short-lived as it was torpedoed and sunk on 16th June that year. Photographs taken after 1972 show it without the nameplates and left simply with the telltale bolt-holes to betray where the plates had once been fitted. The locomotive was eventually preserved several years after its withdrawal from active BR duty on 13th January 1985. Steve Carter Collection (D1408)*

However the lower power rating was within the specification for the Type 4 designs at that time and a low-stressed engine could be expected to be very reliable in traffic. Indeed, for several years the LMS-designed locomotives (10000-1) and their Southern counterparts (10201-3) had covered almost twice the annual mileage of comparable steam engines with this same configuration.

From the overall order for 174 locomotives placed with various companies, the BTC placed an order for ten with English Electric who in turn commenced construction very quickly thereafter at the Vulcan Foundry Works. The frames of the first one, D200 began to come together in 1956 and it was completed in early March 1958. After it was accepted, arrangements were made for a press launch when D200 was allocated to Stratford shed (30A) on the 14th March 1958. The independent locomotive manufacturers would have seen the need to get their products into service as soon as possible, as the BTC was clearly not going to wait much longer before awarding contracts for construction of many more locomotives.

By the September of that year, the first batch of ten locomotives were all in traffic and allocated to the Eastern Region of British Railways; working from either London's Stratford (30A) and Hornsey (34B) engine sheds, mostly on former Great Eastern Railway routes. The following summer of 1959 was to see follow-on orders to the same original design arriving at regular intervals, with allocations to the London Midland Region (LMR) as well as the ER.

Deliveries of the subsequent batches averaged over one per month from Vulcan Foundry, which built numbers D200 to D304. However the success of English Electric's sales force in winning an order for 22 production Deltics (covered in Volume Three), meant that the factory's manufacturing capacity was exceeded. A decision was therefore made to transfer the next batch of Type 4s (D305-D324) to the Robert Stephenson & Hawthorn's Works in Darlington.

Above: *Another EE Type 4 that commemorated a former Cunard liner was D214* Antonia, *which is seen here as 214 at Edge Hill. It was named on 24th May 1961 at Derby Works, but it most likely lost its nameplates during the re-paint into blue livery. It became 40014 in 1973 and spent most of its working days based in Manchester. It was withdrawn and stored at Reddish from 9th November 1981, before being quickly moved on to join the massed ranks of redundant locomotives assembled at Swindon Works on 22nd February 1982. It then lingered around the Works for many months but was finally cut up by November 1983. The Cunard liner after which it was called was built by Vickers Limited in their yard at Barrow-in-Furness during 1921, for the busy trans-Atlantic routes from Liverpool, Southampton and Greenock. It was also converted into an Armed Merchant Cruiser in 1940 but it was then purchased by the Admiralty in March 1942 who converted it to the repair ship* Wayland, *which was finally scrapped at Troon in 1948. Steve Ireland Collection (D1409)*

Above: *Named Type 4s on the southern stretch of the East Coast Main Line were not common. As a consequence this photograph at Hadley Wood of 40015 Aquitania (D215) on a relief service to Kings Cross on Friday 4th September 1981, is noteworthy. The locomotive was withdrawn on 13th November 1984 and was to become one of the last handful of Class 40s to be cut up at Swindon before the works closed in November 1986. The locomotive had been named at Crewe Works in May 1962 when it was almost three years old after another Cunard liner. Built in 1913 the* Aquitania *was built by John Brown & Co. Limited at Clydebank. The vessel only managed to make three voyages before the outbreak of World War I, when it was fitted out as an Armed Merchant Cruiser, before becoming a troopship and later a hospital ship. After the war it resumed commercial work and in October 1931 it made the very first North Atlantic turnaround in two weeks. In World War II it assumed the role of a troopship again and by the time of its scrapping at Faslane in 1950, it had 443 round trips of the North Atlantic to its credit.* Colin Whitbread (D1410)

These were the last to be built with the headcode discs and gangway doors. When building resumed at Vulcan Foundry in 1961, the need for discs had been dropped in favour of Alpha-numeric roller blinds behind glass panels. The next batch (D325-D344) adopted the style used on the contemporary Peaks, which had one two-digit box on either side of the nose cone doors.While these split-headcode Type 4s were being constructed it must have been decided that the nose cone doors and gangways were no longer needed. Accordingly. the final batch (D345-D399) were built with a single-piece four-character headcode box design.

As the Type 4s were to be used on passenger trains, they had to be fitted with train heating equipment. This was provided by one or other of the two types of water boilers fitted to the class; D200-259/267-286/305-324 carried Stone-Vapor type whilst D260-266/287-304/325-399 were fitted with Clayton boilers, although D255 was built with an early form of Electric Train Supply (ETS).

The experience of the BR running department(s) showed the design was too under-powered for its own weight, which was quoted in the BR *Engine Driver's Manual* and the *Ian Allan Combined ABC* of 1959 at 133-tons and elsewhere as 136-tons. This resulted in a few embarrassing incidents with steam locomotives helping them out over the summits at Grayrigg, Shap and Beattock on the West Coast Main Line (WCML).

Aside from the elimination of steam from the railways, the BTC, and from 1962 its successor the British Railways Board (BRB), wanted to decrease journey times between major cities to attract custom away from the increasing use of cars on our roads. The only way this could be done was either by a) reducing the loading of the trains; or b) through lightening the weight of the train by removing a couple of coaches; or increasing the power by double-heading locomotives, which would hardly be economic.

Below: *Here we see 40016 (D216) under the wires at Crewe after it had been renumbered into the TOPS sequences in November 1973. Initially D216 went into service on 27th June 1959 and after an initial period at Crewe shed it was re-allocated to Carlisle Upperby (12B). Then in May 1962 the locomotive was awarded the name* Campania *in Crewe Works but without any ceremony. It resumed activity on trains from Carlisle for another couple of years before a spell as a pool locomotive with the allocation London North Western Lines (LNWL). For the next few years this pattern of activity saw the locomotive, like many classmates, shuffling around the depots of the North West. Its namesake was built as long ago as 1893 by Fairfield shipyard at Govan and had been scheduled for retirement in 1914. It was briefly returned to service and later converted to an armed merchant cruiser with a flight deck and hangar, becoming the HMS* Campania *in April 1916. Adrian Healey/Steve Ireland Collection (D1411)*

Above: *To protect them from cold weather extra frost grilles were fitted to the Class 40s at various times, although these were often removed in later years, as can be seen on 40017. This locomotive had entered service as D217 in July 1959 and was sent to Longsight (9A) after its acceptance trials. In 1960 a spell of seven months followed at Camden (1B), and this was just part of the numerous allocation changes it had in its first ten years! In May 1962 D217 was named* Carinthia *in Crewe Works and it is seen here near Barrow Hill on 28th January 1979. It was not withdrawn until 1st February 1981 after which it was cut up at Swindon Works in August 1981. Built for Cunard by John Brown & Company Limited in Glasgow in 1955, the RMS* Carinthia *was one of four almost identical vessels, but as trade diminished it was only in service with Cunard for 11 years!* Ian Harrison (D1412)

A decision was therefore taken to place future orders in the Type 4 classification with an improved power-to-weight ratio. It is in this decision that we see the contribution made by the Falcon Works of Brush Electrical Engineering Co. Limited at Loughborough. Their new Type 4, later the Class 47s would be built in much greater numbers than any of the earlier designs.

An option of course would have been to acquire more EE Type 5s, but whilst the superior power of the Deltic was undoubtedly attractive, they had a much higher capital cost than was available in the budget. Perhaps if DP2 with its Deltic body-shell and up-rated engine, had been created a little earlier than 1962, Brush would have had a stronger challenge when it came to tendering for the bulk of the Type 4 orders from the BRB.

Top Right: *The end of the line for 40018 (D218 Carmania) came in August 1983. Based at Springs Branch, Wigan for its last seven years of service, it was withdrawn on 14th September 1981 and sent to Crewe Works for storage pending scrapping. However, the end was not yet and 40018 was stored outside Crewe Diesel Depot between January and 15th September 1982, when it was sent to Derby Works for further storage. On 24th June 1984 it was again returned to Crewe and finally scrapped at the works a couple of months later. The ship after which it was named was built by John Brown in 1905 and was used in Cunard's North Atlantic fleet although it served as an armed merchant cruiser, then troopship during World War I.*
Steve Ireland Collection (D1413)

Bottom Right: *Another of the Cunard liners to donate its name was the RMS Caronia, and this was awarded to D219 at Crewe Works in June 1962. This was the second ship of that name, and had been launched on 30th October 1947. The locomotive's nameplates seem to have been removed around 1971, well before being re-numbered to 40019 in 1973. It was allocated mainly around the North West, however, in this view 40019 is storming past Haymarket depot on 5th April 1980, and is seen carrying a painted name. After withdrawal the locomotive was sent initially to Crewe Works in January 1982, but then transferred to Doncaster Works on 24th June 1983. Final cutting took place by BREL staff during February 1984.*
Strathwood Library Collection
(D1414)

Top Left: *The EE Type 4 D220 was delivered new in July 1959 and named* Franconia *at Crewe Works on 16th February 1963. We see the locomotive here at the entrance to Crewe Diesel Depot as 220 on 4th August 1973, after British Rail had decided to dispense with the 'D' prefix once steam locomotives had been removed from the system. It had already lost its plates before being re-numbered 40020 in 1973, but it would last until 1987 when it would be scrapped at Crewe Works. By the time D220 was named the RMS* Ivernia *had undergone a major re-fit to emerge as the third Cunard vessel to be called* Franconia *in January 1963. It seems that the locomotive lost its nameplates in late 1971, around the same time as the liner was sold to the Russians who renamed it the* Fedor Shalyapin. *Roger Bradley (D1415)*

Bottom Left: *During the planned run-down of the class, 40021 (D221* Ivernia*) was the first casualty. It was withdrawn on 17th July 1976, having already been laid up at Reddish since April of that year. It moved to BREL's Crewe Works during October 1976 and was quickly processed in the Melt Shop in May 1977 after a working life of just 17 years. This view of 40021, taken in the dusk at Guide Bridge on 10th December 1975, shows the scars where its nameplates were formerly located. The RMS* Ivernia *(II) was the second Cunard ship to carry the name, but (as seen above) it was later re-named* Franconia *(III).*
Steve Ireland Collection (D1416)

Top Right: *Our research suggests that the only Class 40 to remain in green and still carry its nameplates after being re-numbered was 40022* Laconia *(formerly D222). It is seen here against the light at Holyhead on 21st July 1974. Under the TOPS scheme the locomotive was allocated its new number in 1973, though its actual re-numbering was reported as being in April 1974. Whilst 40010/17/18/31 and 35 all survived in green before re-numbering under the TOPS, it is widely believed that they had all been robbed of their nameplates by that time. Two Cunard ships have carried the name* Laconia *but D222 was named after* Laconia *(II), which was launched in 1921 and lost in a tragic incident on 12th September 1942. Steve Ireland Collection (D1417)*

Bottom Right: *This photograph shows D223 at Willesden Shed (1A) on 20th September 1959, with another all-green EE Type 4 behind. On 19th May 1961 it was named* Lancastria *at Derby Works after a vessel originally built as the RMS* Tyrrhenia *by William Beardmore & Co. in 1920. Its maiden voyage was made on the Glasgow-Canada run on 13th June 1922, but two years later it was given a refit to work the New York services and re-named* Lancastria. *On 17th June 1940 it was sunk whilst trying to evacuate members of the British Expeditionary Force from St. Nazaire during the Dunkirk evacuations. The locomotive itself was renumbered 40023 in 1973 under TOPS and was withdrawn to Crewe Works in 1981. Frank Hornby (D1418)*

Above: *Captured in the sun at Kilmarnock, again in 1969, D224 is still displaying its attractive nameplates. Taken into traffic at Crewe North (5A) on 15th August 1959 before being sent to Camden (1B), it took on the name of the 1893-built Lucania at Crewe Works in August 1962. Aside from a month on loan to York in 1970 it was always an LMR-allocated locomotive. It was re-numbered to 40024 and withdrawn after a ten-year spell as a Longsight locomotive, on 12th June 1984 it went to the Gresty Lane sidings at Crewe for storage. By November it had entered the BREL Works to be stored amongst lines of other withdrawn locomotives (including fellow Class 40s) before being finally scrapped by September 1985.*
Arthur Wilson (D1419)

Nevertheless, for some of us the EE Type 4s/Class 40s struck a soft spot in their service lives with the attractive nameplates on the earlier locomotives evoking the romance of travel and the sea.

Editor's note: "The BRB's decision to name some of these Modernisation Plan Type 4 locomotives can be explained because a batch of them were intended for the West Coast Main Line, and a decision was taken to name the next 50 locomotives delivered after famous liners that were then sailing from Liverpool: the Southern Railway and its successors had used the names of shipping lines that sailed from Southampton on the Merchant Navy Class steam locomotives the previous decade.

A letter was sent to the Cunard shipping line on 4th June 1956 by the BRB, inviting the company to nominate vessel names for potential inclusion in the list of locomotive names. It is assumed that other shipping companies received a similar letter including the Canadian Pacific Line. Cunard responded with a list of names a month later.

In the end just 25 of the English Electric Type 4 Class (D210-D234) carried the names of ocean-going liners on cast nameplates, signifying the importance of rail passenger workings to and from Liverpool. The list may have been re-visited in due course, as new names were suggested and some older ones were removed as Cunard either withdrew or re-named ships and launched new ones after the original submission. The BRB still adopted some of the names that had disappeared from the Lloyd's Register by 1961-3 for the named 25 locomotives.

Below: A particular favourite with enthusiasts, 40025 (D225 Lusitania) is seen at Stockport on 24th June 1981 on an empty stock working; the second coach in the rake being one from a DMU. Its naming took place on 8th March 1962 inside Crewe Works whilst it was a Longsight (9A) locomotive. However, it lost the original nameplates around 1972, but later displayed a painted version. Taken out of traffic on 18th October 1982, it was dumped at Stratford until February 1983 and then endured a two-year spell in the line of condemned engines at Healey Mills. This was followed by a short trip to Doncaster Works where it was cut up by May 1985. The RMS Lusitania had been built by John Brown and launched on 7th June 1906, but was sunk off the Old Head of Kinsale in Ireland with the loss of 1,198 souls on 7th May 1915. The loss of the ship was material in bringing the United States of America into World War I in 1917 on the side of the British Empire and its allies. Colin Whitbread (D1420)

Below: *D226 (later renumbered 40026) entered service at Crewe North (5A) on 22nd August 1959, before it was sent to Camden (1B) in October 1959. It stayed there for the next six years until a transfer to Bescot (2F) in December 1965. Throughout this period it was nameless, but was intended that the locomotive would carry the name* Media *after a Cunard vessel built by John Brown. Launched in 1946, this vessel made its maiden voyage on 20th August 1947. The locomotive was based in Manchester for the rest of its working life but was 'stored' from January to April 1976. It was then taken back into service as seen here in this shot at Guide Bridge on 11th August 1978, where the engine is running light. It worked on until 24th August 1980, before joining the lines of condemned locomotives at Swindon Works and finally cut-up in September 1983.*
Steve Ireland Collection (D1421)

As stated, the first of the English Electric Type 4s (D200) entered traffic in early 1958, but towards the end of their revenue-earning careers they had become the Class 40s and were nicknamed 'Whistlers' as a result of their distinctive sound. They had also acquired a loyal following of enthusiasts, all keen to experience as much as they could of 'Whistler' haulage and this support has continued with the active privately-owned survivors.

I hope that you will enjoy this selection of images from the Strathwood Library and that you will be encouraged to make contact with us, perhaps to add duplicate slides to enhance your own collection. A special thank you should be extended for the invaluable help and assistance from Steve Ireland and Colin Whitbread.

David Hayward & Kevin Derrick   May 2005

Top Right: *Also seen at Guide Bridge, is 40027 on 2nd October 1979. It went in to traffic at Longsight (9A) on 23rd August 1959 as D227, and was named* Parthia *at Crewe Works on 23rd June 1962. It spent most of its service days around Manchester, finally being withdrawn from Longsight on 25th April 1983. It moved to Crewe Works a week later and was dealt with by the cutters during the following April. The ship, RMS* Parthia *was the second Cunard liner of that name, and the sister of the* Media. *It was built by Harland & Wolff Limited in Belfast and made its maiden voyage on 10th April 1948; it made its final sailing for Cunard on 23rd September 1961 before being sold to a New Zealand company.* Colin Whitbread (D1422)

Bottom Right: *Here 40028 (D228)* Samaria *is found at Lowton near Wigan on 5th May 1982. By this time, several of the Class 40s had seen their original numbers restored by depot staff. The name* Samaria *has also been repainted on its sides but less lavishly so than other members of the Class. The locomotive was withdrawn in 1984 and was scrapped by Crewe Works. The Cunard ship* Samaria *was the second ship of that name, and was built by Cammell Laird at Birkenhead and launched in 1920, before making its maiden voyage on 19th April 1922. In 1939 it was converted into a troop ship, and finally returned to Cunard in 1950. A year later, after a full refit it resumed trans-Atlantic sailings until early 1956* Leonard Ball (D1423)

Above: *The use of the Class 40s on passenger workings along the North Wales Coast during the summer months, as 40029 is illustrated at Rhyl on Saturday 29th July 1978 whilst engaged on the 11.18 Crewe to Llandudno service. The locomotive was originally numbered D229 and then named* Saxonia *in Crewe Works on 11th September 1962. When renumbered under TOPS as 40029, it joined the other Longsight-allocated named Class 40s. It stayed at this Manchester depot until 25th April 1984 when it was posted as withdrawn. Stored briefly at Basford Hall Sidings, Crewe for a few months, it progressed to Doncaster Works on 31st July 1984, and had been scrapped by November that year. The liner it was named after, the RMS Saxonia was the second Cunard vessel of this name and was launched from the John Brown shipyard on Clydebank as part of a quartet of almost identical ships. It made its maiden voyage from Liverpool to Québec and Montréal on 2nd September 1954, but in 1957 route changes saw it being moved to the Southampton-Canada service. Saxonia was extensively re-fitted for cruising during the winter of 1962-63, re-named* Carmania *and painted a two-tone light green, as with other Cunard vessels used for this purpose.* Colin Whitbread (D1424)

18

Below: *Taking on fuel at Wigan Spring's Branch on 26th September 1982, 40030 (D230 Scythia) is adding further to its considerable weight as its tanks held 710-gallons of diesel. When new from English Electric in 1959 it went to Carlisle Upperby (12B) as its first shed, quickly being re-allocated to Crewe North (5A). It was taken to Derby Works for a naming ceremony on 8th April 1961, adopting the name of another Cunard ship. Scrapping occurred in 1983 at BREL Crewe Works. The second Cunard ship with the name Scythia was built by Vickers at Barrow and launched on 23rd April 1920, before entering service on the busy routes from Liverpool to New York and Boston 20th August 1921. During World War II it saw active service as a troopship, and was later used to both repatriate German POWs and carry German emigrants to Canada under charter by the International Refugee Organisation until 1948. After its return to Cunard in 1949, the liner underwent a substantial refit and then resumed commercial voyages on the Liverpool- Québec route in 1950, as well as sailings from London and Southampton. In October 1957 Scythia was chartered to the Canadian government for service between Rotterdam to Québec and then its last Atlantic crossing was just before Christmas 1957, after which it passed to Wards of Inverkeithing for scrapping in the New Year.*
Steve Ireland Collection (D1425)

Below: *This photograph of 40031 (D231 Sylvania) shows the last pieces being dealt with by the scrapmen at the Melt Shop in Crewe Works during an organised enthusiast's visit on 21st May 1983. When new the locomotive had been sent first to Crewe shed in September 1959, and subsequently named in the works in May 1962. The same workshops would carry out much of its overhaul work in the ensuing years and it would eventually meet its end as seen here. Having been a Longsight locomotive until 31st May 1981, it had been named after the RMS Sylvania, which was Cunard's second vessel of that name, and sister to* Saxonia (II), Carinthia, *and* Ivernia (II); *like them, it was built by John Brown.*

Launched in 1956, it made its maiden voyage on 5th June 1957 from Greenock to Montréal. The Sylvania *and its three sister ships then maintained a weekly service to Canada from Liverpool and Southampton until 1961.* Sylvania *then replaced the recently-retired* Britannic (III) *on the Liverpool-New York service. It later earned the distinction of making Cunard's final regularly scheduled sailings to Canada, as well as the final Cunard passenger sailing from Liverpool to North America on 30th November 1967. It was then used only for cruising until Cunard sold the vessel to the Sitmar line in 1968 who re-named it* Fairwind.

Steve Ireland Collection (D1426)

Above: *With all of the sailings to Canada among the liners mentioned so far, it is perhaps no surprise that there was a vessel named* Empress of Canada. *The name was taken up by D232 on 17th March 1961 at Derby Works, after the third Canadian Pacific line ship of that name. Canadian Pacific's final transatlantic liner,* Empress of Canada *was built by Vickers-Armstrong (Shipbuilders) Limited at Walker-on-Tyne. Launched in May 1960, it made its maiden voyage from Liverpool to Montréal on 24th April 1961, a few weeks after the namesake locomotive's ceremony. Throughout its career* Empress of Canada *was used for cruising as well as trans-Atlantic service, but in March 1970 it became Canadian Pacific's only surviving trans-Atlantic liner. Ultimately, on 7th November 1971,* Empress of Canada *made Canadian Pacific's final Liverpool-Montréal round trip, which ended on 23rd November. As 40032 and shorn of its nameplates the locomotive is seen at Pensarn with a North Wales coast excursion on 30th May 1978. Sadly the Class 40 was withdrawn in 1981 and scrapped at Swindon Works in April 1983. Aldo Delicata (D1427)*

Above: *Finding colour photographs of Class 40s renumbered and with their nameplates still in situ is not an easy task. However, 40033* Empress of England *(originally D233) is seen in this condition whilst powering a Freightliner train at Holyhead during August 1974. This apparently contradicts the suggestions that both 40032 and 40033 lost their Empress nameplates in 1972 and 1971 respectively, The nameplates on D233 were unveiled in Derby Works on 9th September 1961, some four years after the liner* Empress of England *was built by Vickers-Armstrong (Shipbuilders) Limited at Walker-on-Tyne in 1957. Initially designed for services from Liverpool to Québec and Montréal (in the summer) and St. John (in winter), the diminishing traffic allowed the liner to be used for winter cruises from New York to the Caribbean. As years passed, more of its time was spent cruising as air travel hit the trans-Atlantic market. Initial passenger capacity was 160 First Class and 898 Tourist Class on liner services, but less when cruising. In 1970 the vessel was sold to the Shaw Savill Line, who had ambitious plans to increase their cruising market. The project was doomed almost from the start, as the conversion work at Cammell Laird's stretched to over a year. The vessel eventually re-appeared in October 1971 as the* Ocean Monarch, *but it only operated until 1975, when it was sold for scrap. The locomotive was withdrawn in 1984 and unlike 40032, was scrapped at Doncaster Works.*
Eric McBrine Courtesy Craig McBrine (D1428)

Top Right: *As seen in this view at Colwyn Bay on Saturday 29th July 1978 whilst 40034 was working the 14.30 Crewe to Holyhead train in Rail Blue livery, the scars left behind after its nameplate removal are clearly visible. The locomotive D234 had been named* Accra *at Crewe Works in May 1962 and it was allocated to Rugby (1F) for all of 1965 and into 1966. It was eventually assigned to Longsight (LO) on the LMR, from where it was withdrawn in March 1984 and sent for scrapping at Doncaster Works. The Elder Dempster liner* Accra, *which entered service in September 1947 was the third ship of that name and sister ship to* Apapa (II). *Incorporated into the nameplates were both the pennant and the name of the shipping line concerned as seen on page 59 in more detail.* Colin Whitbread (D1429)

Bottom Right: *Named at the same time as D234, D235 took on the name of the* Apapa, *the sister ship to the* Accra. *Both ships were built by Vickers-Armstrong of Barrow-in-Furness for the Elder Dempster Line's West Africa service as suggested by their names. Here 235 is seen on the WCML in February 1974, whilst running through Lancaster with a parcels working. The location of where its nameplates were once carried is still discernible, as the accumulated grime and staining behind the plate was harder to shift. In 1973 235 was re-numbered 40035 and was finally scrapped at Crewe Works, following withdrawal in 1984.* Arthur Wilson (D1430)

Above: *This photograph has been selected to potentially quell any argument that the clearances were tight between the body and washing plants, which some say required the removal of the namepelates. The width of a Class 40 without nameplates is quoted as nine feet whereas that of the Brush Type 4s, Class 47s (that all-region bench mark) is nine feet two inches without nameplates. The photograph also serves another purpose, showing that some depots such as Haymarket paid attention to locomotive cleaning, as we see 40097 (originally D297) taking a 'wash and brush up' after working in from the LMR on 3rd July 1978, Ultimately it was derailment damage that caught out this particular Class 40, and it was put into storage at Holyhead (HD) in May 1983. Officially withdrawn from stock on 26th June 1983 it went to Crewe for seven months before moving again to the Doncaster Works. Cutting-up work began on 1st February 1984, and all traces of it had gone by the end of March 1984.*
Adrian Healey/Steve Ireland Collection (D1431)

Below: *Demonstrating the second type of nose and headcode treatment in some style is 40140, formerly D340, along with fellow Class 40 40033 (Empress of England) with a Class 25 25173 sandwiched between them. This trio is seen with just seven MkI coaches in tow at Prestatyn on 30th May 1981, presumably 40033 had failed and its classmate was added as the Class 25 was deemed insufficient to take the load. Interestingly, 40140 has lost its frost grilles along the side air intakes and appears to be carrying a faded red buffer beam under some of the grime. The 1961-built locomotive was withdrawn in 1982 and subsequently scrapped at Crewe.* Steve Ireland Collection (D1432)

Above: *Displaying the final factory option of nose style with a central headcode panel is 40185 , which is found at Liverpool Lime Street on 29th April 1978 having arrived with a North West Rambler Railtour from Euston. This locomotive was delivered in 1962 as D385, and was withdrawn in 1983. This picture is an apt place to clarify the exact numbers that were* built with each type of nose design; originally there were 124 locomotives with disc headcodes; 22 as split-headcodes, whilst the remaining 54 took on the style above. These were to change after entry into service as many locomotives had subsequent modifications carried out, as we will discuss shortly.
Colin Whitbread (D1433)

LIVERY VARIATIONS

Over the years, the Type 4/Class 40s were to sport a number of livery variations, but Brunswick Green and Rail Blue were the primary base colours. As the last of this type (D399) entered traffic at Gateshead (52A) on 5th September 1962, the majority entered service in all-over green livery. The majority also had a light grey relief band along the cant rail, red buffer beams and silvered buffers. A number of the early engines carried a ladder fixed to the front of the nose cone. This was to assist the crew and cleaning staff to reach the central windscreen, although they were quickly removed for operational reasons and not just because of the electrification concerns.

Below: *D251 still has its ladder in place when seen on Cocksburnpath Bank. It seems to be on an express working, judging from the arrangement of the discs, which were placed to coincide with the traditional lamp placing on steam locomotives. Situated on the former North British Railway main line from Berwick-upon-Tweed to Edinburgh, the station here closed in 1951. The gradient was 1 in 96 for just over four miles and was a popular spot for photographers in steam days, although it is a pity that more people did not film the early diesels. As a result, and because of their apparent scarcity, it is always a pleasure to discover 'new' transparencies from this era. Under the TOPS scheme D251 was renumbered as 40051, and the locomotive was finally withdrawn in 1978 before being scrapped at Doncaster Works.* Noel Marrison (D1434)

Below: *One of the delights found in some images from the 1960s are the semaphore signals such as these former Great Western Railway upper quadrants. Another sign of those long-past times is the standard half-yellow pattern of warning panel that began to appear on diesel and electric locomotives from 1962. These were introduced on the last deliveries from the makers when the concept was approved, but was (as soon as was practicable) retrospectively applied to the entire fleet of English Electric Type 4s. During the mid- and late-1960s, EE Type 4s could be seen with regular goods train workings down to Banbury, Oxford and Reading, so the sight of D290 here at Leamington Spa was not out of place by any means. The headcode suggests that this is an express freight not fitted with a continuous brake, so the dead weight of a Class 40 would be useful descending the nearby Hatton Bank in one direction to Leamington Spa and from Lapworth in the other. According to various sources, number 365 (formerly D365 and subsequently 40165) was possibly the last survivor with the half-yellow front livery in 1972. In 1973, D290 was re-numbered 40090 under TOPS but withdrawal came in 1981 followed by scrapping at Doncaster Works.*

Tim Meredith (D1435)

Above: *Although it has previously been published that Crewe Works were responsible for out-shopping D216, 240, 241, 242, 243, 261 and D270 into an early Rail Blue re-paint in the style of D206 on the cover, some of these may have been re-painted in various depots. Alternatively, some may have been done at Glasgow Works, as they were certainly turning out Clayton Type 1 locomotives in Rail Blue at this time. The author recollects scenes such as this one of an ex-works EE Type 4, which is either being re-painted into green again or just given a respectable touch-up inside Crewe Works on 20th August 1967, illustrating the point that the green was not to the same standard of finish as the new all yellow fronts. This view, taken while the paint dried, also serves as a reminder of how many access doors had to be sealed to prevent the ingress of draughts to the cabs. The smartly painted cast shed plate is neatly done underneath the number D209 showing Carlisle Kingmoor (12A). Despite this plate, in theory it was allocated to LNWL rather than any specific shed at this time, having just completed a stint of four months allocated to Ipswich (32B). Prior to this it had been in the care of Stratford (30A) since October 1961 and this was its first allocation to the LMR. It then had ten further allocation code changes before being cut-up at Doncaster Works in 1985, being renumbered in 1973 as 40009.* Frank Hornby (D1436)

Above: *Although many of the fleet of green EE Type 4s were seen in an unkempt state after steam ended in 1968, many enthusiasts were happy to still see green engines no matter what condition they were in. Here we see number 333 (formerly D333, built in 1961 and withdrawn as 40133 in 1984) alongside Crewe Depot in 1972, awaiting its next journey back north. The policy of not immediately re-painting the green engines has to be considered against the numbers of locomotives in the class and the capacity of the Crewe Works to patch up Type 1s, 3s and 4s in the early 1970s. A large number of green locomotives thus lasted long enough to attract modern traction enthusiasts coming into the hobby years after the introduction of Rail Blue, a colour scheme that was hated by many at the time but one that is missed today. Small numbers of coaches and parcels stock also remained in the complimentary maroon livery until the mid-1970s as well, so green locomotives and maroon stock could also be seen together from time to time. This continued in some cases even after the introduction of TOPS and many years before privately-owned stock was allowed to run on BR. It appears that the last of the Class 40s to retain their old style numbers were 265, 358, 362 and 364, reportedly re-numbered on the 14th September 1974 as 40065/158/162 and 40164 respectively.*
Steve Carter Collection (D1437)

30

Below: *It is thought that as many as 34 of the class survived to be re-numbered under TOPS whilst still wearing British Railways green livery: although Russell Saxton quotes the definitive list as 40010, 7, 8, 22, 31, 35, 39, 52, 87, 88 and 96 then 40101, 104, 106, 115, 133, 135-9, 145, 153, 169, 171, 176, 180-4, 187 and 199. Among these was 40096, which we can now see entering Falkland Yard with a rake of 16-ton coal wagons in May 1974. The locomotive, formerly D296, was finally withdrawn in 1983 and subsequently scrapped at Doncaster Works.* Arthur Wilson (D1438)

Above: *Although D200 was re-painted green after reinstatement, the last British Rail-owned mainline locomotive to remain in Brunswick Green livery (having supposedly never having been re-painted in blue), was classmate 40106 (D306). It thus became a celebrity locomotive long before the pioneer, however EE Type 1 20141 was the last surviving main line green loco in normal service and was still in this colour scheme in May 1980. Although 40106 was only fitted with vacuum brakes, it had managed to avoid being taken out of service even though several others thus fitted had already been withdrawn. Here we see 40106 at St. Pancras on 28th April 1979. It was working a special train when the photographer pictured it venturing back out into the rain during a light engine movement. To this day there have been persistent rumours that suggest 40106 was re-painted (at least into undercoat for blue) during its Works visit to Crewe in 1978, before it was decided that both its status and its revenue-earning potential would be lost if the work proceeded. In the event the locomotive was returned to traffic in green and was selected by BR for special duties and railtours. It then took part in the 'Rocket 150' celebrations at Rainhill, in May 1980. It was withdrawn from BR traffic on 21st April 1983, being deemed 'life-expired'. The pioneer, D200, had by then been restored to operational condition, and became the replacement for 40106 on special passenger duties. D306 was subsequently bought by Gerald Boden in March 1984.* Colin Whitbread (D1439)

Below: *Among the first things to strike you in this view at Newcastle Central on 9th December 1980, is the shiny finish of the locomotive's grey roof under the station lighting. This level of finish on the bonnet of 40106 would have been a distraction to the engine crew, so a subtle matt black patch was applied and this had been extended over the yellow since the previous picture was taken. With Longsight responsible for its maintenance, the locomotive enjoyed celebrity status until officially withdrawn. However as with the best of celebrities it had enjoyed a final encore and made appearances at exhibitions like that held at Wrexham General Station in September 1983.*

After its sale, 40106 was unloaded onto Great Central Railway metals on 18th April 1984, the 26th anniversary of D200's inaugural working from London Liverpool Street. In October 1987 the locomotive was used for the railway scenes in the 1988 movie Buster, which told the story of the 1963 Great Train Robbery and starred the rock legend Phil Collins. The film was shot on location at the Great Central Railway and a special second track was laid for the purposes of authenticity. The locomotive was also fitted with 'dummy' split-headcode panels and given the number D326, the actual Class 40 used in the robbery. Colin Whitbread (D1441)

Above: *Canning Street North Junction on 16th February 1985. saw a special working behind pioneer D200, or 40122 (the number allocated under TOPS in the absence of the aforementioned accident victim D322). The survival of 40122 had not been a foregone conclusion at all, despite the fact that it should have been a candidate for the National Collection. Likewise, the Class 40 Preservation Society, while wishing to save the pioneer, could not justify the funds from their membership at the time. After the locomotive was withdrawn it was placed in store at Kingmoor until April 1983, where it was not far from the salt air blowing in from the Solway Firth and as a result it began to deteriorate rapidly. Like many preservation attempts, its salvation only came at the last moment and almost when it was too late.*

Fortunately a campaign was started by modern traction magazine RAIL Enthusiast, *and this was supported by the Association of Railway Preservation Societies. Further lobbying went right to the top and British Rail's Chairman, Sir Peter Parker took an interest and this ultimately brought about success. Initially it helped to ensure that 40122 was not hauled away to Swindon Works and scrapped, but it also meant that 40106 could be withdrawn at a time when it was not even five years past its last works overhaul and still had vacuum-only train brakes. To keep costs to a minimum, the restoration work on D200 was carried out as an apprentice training programme at Toton TMD, using withdrawn 40076 as a 'donor' loco for its power unit and bogies.*
Steve Ireland Collection (D1442)

Below: *The reinstated locomotive re-entered traffic in April 1983, painted in original Dark Brunswick green livery with full yellow ends, numbered both D200 and 40122. Fortunately, during the repainting work, it was arranged that the engine could be pictured with a green nose, followed by a half-yellow warning panel and finally with full-yellow panel, all three versions being printed in* RAIL Enthusiast *accordingly. The locomotive's condition was excellent, which in itself was a tribute to the enthusiasm, care and hard work done by everyone at Toton. After the restoration and return to service, D200 was assigned to special duties such as enthusiast railtour trains. The locomotive was also used for general freight and passenger traffic in the Carlisle area where a regular turn was the daily out-and-back Carlisle to Leeds passenger train. This helped bring much needed income and publicity to the famous Settle & Carlisle route at a time when it was being proposed for closure. D200 was finally withdrawn and handed over to the NRM at York on 16th April 1988. Unfortunately the other Class 40, 40062 (D262) that was stored at Kingmoor with 40122 after withdrawal in 1981 was not reprieved, and was condemned to its fate at Swindon Works in June 1983.* Steve Ireland Collection (D1443)

Above: *The excellent restoration of D200/40122 allowed photographers to recreate some of those early publicity images once more, with a little imagination. When new to service in March 1958 D200 had been allocated to Stratford (30A) and among its early task was a publicity picture, which declared 'FIRST 2000hp Diesel LONDON-NORWICH progress by GREAT EASTERN'. Almost 30 years later a very similar headboard was placed on the restored locomotive, but slightly higher this time in order not to obscure the yellow warning panel. The re-created picture, taken near Bethnal Green, makes* a pretty picture but the scene in the background gives away the passage of time. During the period while D200's rescue was being orchestrated, Class 40s had begun to form long queues for the scrap men to deal with, and as a result the enthusiasm for the remaining Class 40s was very visible now. During 1984 it was clear that the end was nigh, and the start of 1985 saw the withdrawal of the survivors. The NRM agreed to claim the locomotive after all and D200 joined the National Collection on 16th April 1988 when it arrived at York with its 'final' rail tour. Strathwood Library Collection (D1444)

Top Right: *Making an ethereal appearance on 12th March 1988, D200 in undercoat along with Electric Train Heating Locomotive 97250 ETHEL 2 [the former Class 25 25305] between Mirfield and Ravensthorpe & Thornhill Junction. The town of Mirfield also boasted its own engine shed which was coded 25D until September 1956 when it became 56D under the North Eastern Region. This was predominantly a freight engine shed that closed to steam on 2nd January 1967, but it did see English Electric Type 3 and Type 4 diesels being based there at odd times, especially between January and April that year (when it closed completely) at which time it was used as a stabling point for visiting diesels.*
Nick Gledhill *(D1445)*

Bottom Right: *On a foggy morning at Didcot on 24th October 1987 we find 40135 (formerly D335), one of the final batch of Class 40s that were used for the remodelling of the mass of pointwork at Crewe in the summer of 1985. It was taken out of service in January 1985 and had already passed to Doncaster Works when it was reinstated during the spring of 1985. Along with 40012, 40060 and 40118, 40135 were 'patched up' and re-entered departmental service for restricted working as 97407/5/8/6 respectively. Final withdrawal for 97406 came on 16th December 1986, but further intervention prevented the locomotive from reaching Swindon Works for scrapping and it was duly preserved.*
Steven Feltham *(D1446)*

Top Left: *The earliest version of the blue livery for the EE Type 4s can be seen on the front cover, showing the early numbering style and the smaller Inter-City arrows. Indeed, there seems to have been little consistency in size of arrows used. However, was 40157 (D357) seen here on 1st March 1980 at Haymarket, unique in not having any arrows on the Rail Blue livery at this time? This locomotive unfortunately suffered a terminal engine room fire just north of Carstairs when in charge of the Stirling-Euston Motorail on 9th July 1983. On 13th August it was hauled south to Doncaster Works who had demolished it by the end of October 1983. A service life of almost 22 years had been mostly spent in Scotland.* Leonard Ball (D1447)

Bottom Left: *When 313 (later 40113) was photographed in the sun on 20th May 1972 nobody would have then imagined that Gateshead Depot (52A) would close. It had long been associated with busy ECML trains, even though its reputation for turning out 'dirty' engines was widely known. The depot had at the time its own stud of EE Type 4s and would often host others from Haymarket, Liverpool, Manchester and York as well. On this late spring day it plays host to this clean blue example from the Manchester Division (D09), most likely Longsight Depot. The locomotive was withdrawn in 1981 and ultimately was despatched to Swindon Works for the inevitable cutting-up in January 1984.* Frank Hornby (D1448)

Above: *It was not solely the preserve of the green Class 40 40106 to run enthusiasts' specials during the late 1970s. For example, on Saturday 11th February 1978, DAA Railtours chartered 40173 (D373) for an extensive tour of the Southern Region. It took the locomotive to some locations where the Class had rarely been seen before, with the possible exception of troop train workings. As can be seen 40173 has been spruced up for the occasion even though it was allocated to far-away Haymarket at the time. Although the general use of headcodes was (to an extent) obsolete by this date, the locomotive is carrying the code 1Z03 with the Z denoting the working as a special. After its coming out of service on 28th August 1981, 40173 was dumped at Eastfield until July 1983.*

Looking the worse for its experiences it then went to Dunfermline Townhill Depot, which had recently closed. Sometime later in 1983 it travelled further north and took up residence in the National Carriers yard in Perth, where it was apparently used as a classroom! By the early part of 1984 it was a sorry mess indeed, stripped of its bogies and many fittings; as virtually just a shell it stood on blocks awaiting its destiny. Ironically it would provide us with another link back to class members named after the ocean liners, as it would be uniquely broken up by Thomas W. Ward of Inverkeithing who had finished off several of the liners as well as many steam locomotives during the 1960s.

Colin Whitbread (D1449)

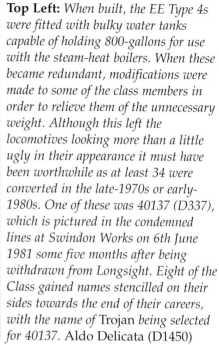

Top Left: *When built, the EE Type 4s were fitted with bulky water tanks capable of holding 800-gallons for use with the steam-heat boilers. When these became redundant, modifications were made to some of the class members in order to relieve them of the unnecessary weight. Although this left the locomotives looking more than a little ugly in their appearance it must have been worthwhile as at least 34 were converted in the late-1970s or early-1980s. One of these was 40137 (D337), which is pictured in the condemned lines at Swindon Works on 6th June 1981 some five months after being withdrawn from Longsight. Eight of the Class gained names stencilled on their sides towards the end of their careers, with the name of* Trojan *being selected for 40137.* Aldo Delicata (D1450)

Bottom Left: *Seen broadside after the water tank's removal, we find 40145 (D345) at Warrington on 28th May 1982. This particular locomotive had spent most of its working life on the Eastern Region, only moving to Longsight in May 1978. Its withdrawal would come about after being derailed in Stourton Yard, Leeds in May 1983. It was taken to Crewe for assessment, but this was not favourable and it was withdrawn a fortnight later on 10th June 1983. Nevertheless, it was to become the target for the Class 40 Preservation Society and it was moved to Bury Transport Museum on 18th February 1984 as the first Class 40 to enter preservation.*
Leonard Ball (D1451)

Above: *A further experiment was carried out to 40069 (D269), but this again did nothing to improve its looks, as the lower skirting was cut away along its body side to allow easier access to the pipe work and plating within. The oil drainage pipes were then accessible to Depot staff from the outside. Because of the extra work required and the fact that capital expenditure on the Class was now frowned upon, it was fortunately an isolated experiment. Even when standing at a platform this disfigurement could be seen. This is demonstrated at Chester on a rainy Saturday lunchtime with 40069 in charge of the 09.08 Scarborough to Llandudno service on 14th June 1980.*

For many years Chester had been a hot spot for Class 40 activity and whilst the depot did not have an allocation of the class, as it was mainly responsible for DMUs, very often one or two 40s could be found resting there. This locomotive was one of those that had many allocations during its service days (20 to be exact), taking in a variety of locations in the ER and LMR. Sent to Longsight for its last nine months, 40069 was dumped at Newton Heath after withdrawal in the autumn of 1983. On 13th December it was sent to BREL Doncaster Works who completed the cutting-up by September 1984.
Colin Whitbread (D1452)

Below: *The nose ends of many of the Class 40s were to be altered at various times from the mid 1970s. Once the headcode discs were no longer in use several locomotives had them removed in an attempt to smarten up the front ends, most likely induced by the need to replace them as the hinges corroded. One such example was 40003 (D203) seen here in a traditional railway setting at Shrewsbury on 18th April 1981. Others noted with their discs removed include 40009 (D209, withdrawn 1984) and 40033 (Empress of England). After 40003 was withdrawn it went from Healey Mills to Stratford for component recovery in order to help ailing class members, as well as to provide spares for Class 50s where these were interchangeable. Famous for their dead weight, this locomotive was to see itself put to good use in Yorkshire for bridge load testing in April 1983, having been taken from Stratford where it had been rotting for six months. Staying in Yorkshire it was then towed to BREL Doncaster Works to keep their cutters in work during January 1984. Ian James (D1453)*

Above: *In a picture taken at Swindon Works on 2nd April 1983, we can see the interesting addition of the indicator discs to split-headcode locomotive 40127 (previously D327). Only one other locomotive, 40131 (the former D331, withdrawn 1983), was treated in the same way.*

During the disposal process, and after withdrawal in 1982, asbestos was discovered in 40127 and this delayed the cutting work while it was dealt with correctly. However, it was no stay of execution and the work was completed by October 1983.
Steve Ireland Collection (D1454)

Above: *Just one of the later central-headcode machines, 40158 (D358), came to be fitted with a Deltic-style headcode panel that had been plated-over and given opaque marker lights. This seems to have been applied as a result of accident damage to the 'Number Two End' only and its style is subtly different to 40060 and 40062, which is illustrated in following pages. With a typical coating of oily muck, 40158 displays its modifications whilst engaged on a mixed freight working at Warrington on 28th June 1983. Going into traffic as D358 on 6th September 1961 at Edinburgh Haymarket (then coded 64B), this particular locomotive would stay based in the Scottish capital for another 19- years, however in May 1981 the surviving Class 40s were concentrated on either Kingmoor or Longsight depots. This particular locomotive went to Kingmoor, from where it was withdrawn a week before Christmas 1983. It was taken from Carlisle to Doncaster Works the following July and picked clean by the scrapmen by September 1984.*
Steve Ireland Collection (D1455)

Below: *Our survey of the small batch of locomotives modified from disc headcode and gangway-doored versions to ones with a sealed nose and central headcode begins with 40060. It is pictured at Newcastle Central with the 07.05 –Edinburgh Waverley on a cold and damp Tuesday morning on 9th December 1980. This locomotive, another long-term resident of Haymarket (21 years), was delivered as D260 with headcode discs and all-over green livery on 19th February 1960. Whilst at Haymarket, locomotives D260 to D266 began to acquire modified noses to remove the draughty communicating doors. Because headcodes were still very much in use, (although many Scottish ones were very simple indeed), it was decided they should be modified to match the later-built locomotives. An example of this rounded edge headcode box is modelled for us on 40060. By the time that photograph was taken the canvas roller blinds for the Alpha-numeric codes have been replaced by marker lights seen through 'Domino dots'. After the locomotive left Haymarket it worked at Kingmoor until withdrawn on 22nd January 1985, when the survivors were finally ordered out of traffic. As mentioned earlier it was then officially reinstated to join three classmates for work at Crewe on engineering trains. Renumbered as 97405 as mentioned above it would be the last of the four to be withdrawn in March 1987. Colin Whitbread (D1456)*

Above: *In a second (slightly earlier) view of 40060, we see it had received a different treatment to the engine's headcode panel. Either the glass panel has been painted over, or it has been removed and replaced with a sheet of metal set within the rubber seal that formerly held the glass. Whatever the case this seems to be a unique treatment, which has left the engine without marker lights at a time when such conversions were being actively undertaken (especially on the Peak Class) following the recognition of the safer operation that such lights brought. Perth is where we find 40060 on 2nd July 1979, as we see it entering the city on the line from Dundee and Aberdeen whilst it was engaged on freight work.*
Adrian Healey - Steve Ireland Collection (D1457)

Above: *The Haymarket conversions of 1965 can be illustrated in this view at Kings Cross in September 1965, where D261 has ventured from its Scottish base. Apart from the different and higher application of the yellow warning panel, a careful comparison of the pictures will reveal that the edges of the headcode box is squared rather than rounded. The type of headcode box and this warning panel are the same as those fitted to the Class 23 Baby Deities which had been rebuilt around the same time. Of the Haymarket engines from the original batch of four-digit head code boxes (D360), has also been pictured wearing the same style of warning panel. These changes will of course be of specific interest to railway modellers.*

Peter Gator (D1458)

Above: *In March 1974, number 261 (the 'D' having been painted out on most diesel locomotives after August 1968), was renumbered into the TOPS sequence as 40061. It was certainly painted blue at this time, and comparison against the earlier view on the previous page shows the differences to the headcode box corners. The time-exposure required to get this shot at Dundee has given away the movement of its semaphore signal, and the colour of the spectacle has lost some of its red by showing green for a few seconds. The locomotive crew were waiting for the road to allow them to take up the stock for the 19.38 service to Glasgow Queen Street on 9th December 1980. Both the North British and the Caledonian Railways had locomotive sheds in the city, Tay Bridge and Dundee West.*

When steam ended officially in the area in 1967 it was the less important Dundee West that assumed the role as a diesel stabling point. When built, the Class 40s had a mechanical lubricator in a small housing on the driver's side bogie step, but these were dispensed with from the late 1960s. Later on a number of the Class also lost their inner sets of sandboxes which were removed from their bogies as well. Although locomotive 40060 still displays its blue-star coupling codes, classmates 40060-66, 40148 and 40157-68 (D260-6, 348 and 357-368), all Haymarket based for most of the 1970s, lost their multiple-working equipment from the front buffer beams. In the end 40061 made its way to Crewe Works for breaking up by March 1984. Colin Whitbread (D1459)

Below: *Haymarket Depot, situated in the shadow of Murrayfield Stadium, seems to have fully maintained its own collection of Class 40s and judging by the length of time that most locomotives remained at the Depot, they were very happy with them once they had carried out their modifications. In this view of 262, repainted into blue and possibly shopped at Glasgow Works, we can see that a small repair is still required for the glass missing from one of the locomotive room windows at the Depot on 12th September 1970. Reference has already been made to the frost grilles but in this view they are very clear. During the 1970s the Eastern Region took the view that the removal of these honeycomb grilles would allow an improved airflow through the radiators. The Scottish Region seems to have followed suit, although the maintenance people of the LMR were not so sure, and preferred the theory of improved frost protection. As a result locomotives transferring to the LMR during this period appear to have had the grilles reinstated. Sometime after 1979 they relented and followed suit themselves. As the winter of 1980/1 approached, 40062 (as it had been renumbered in 1973) was transferred south to Kingmoor who gave it work for the next year. Once withdrawn it did not make the move to Swindon Works until the summer of 1982, where it sat in the open until cut-up in June 1983. Comparisons again should be made with those shots over the page to see the difference the appearance of the grilles makes, as well as the headcode modifications.* Frank Hornby (D1460)

Above: *This photograph shows a Class 40 engaged in a little night-time shunting of parcels stock, which was always a feature of any late night visit to busy main line stations. This was still a feature of the evening activity at York on Sunday 2nd September 1979 when 40062 was acting as the station pilot. Note the modifications to the headcode! A few of the early withdrawals of the Class were as a result of collision damage, first being D322. Then on the 6th August 1975, 40189 (D389) from Wigan Springs Branch Depot came into collision with the Coatbridge-Southampton Freightliner at Weaver Junction just to the north of Crewe whilst it was working a Runcorn-Wallerscote tank train. After the repairs required to 40189* were declared uneconomical, it was withdrawn in January 1976 and cut up at Crewe Works the following April. The next numerically, 40190 (D390), suffered a similar collision three weeks after that of 40189. While it was on the 02.00 Uttoxeter-Ellesmere Port tanker train, a collision occurred with the 19.45 service to Liverpool behind 47437. The Crewe cutters set to work on 40190 straight after dealing with 40189 and it was gone by the end of May 1976. The next three to go were 40005, 40039 (still in green) and 40102 now life-expired and surplus to requirements. Steady inroads had thus already been made into the class when this photograph was taken.

Colin Whitbread (D1461)

Below: *Edinburgh's magnificent Waverley Station was built by the North British Railway on a 23-acre site and once had 19 platforms. A view at this station on 13th June 1981 shows another modification to the Class 40s, which in turn contrasts with the previously shown picture of 40069 and its cut-away side panels that were intended to allow easier access to pipe work. On some class members a different approach was taken and as photographs of Class 40s from the later 1970s will show flexible armoured pipe work for oil drainage hanging down. This has been traced to at least 24 locomotives with many of them based in Scotland, amongst which was 40063 (D263). This particular example would manage another three years work south of the border before it was withdrawn on 15th April 1984. It was stored at Bescot for several months until somebody then came up with the idea of naming it Express Link and cleaning it up for exhibitions at Stourbridge and Worcester that autumn. It was sent back to Bescot for the winter until sold and delivered to Vic Berry's yard in Leicester, where it was finally scrapped in June 1987. One other point to note of the differences between locomotives was that the first batches of EE Type 4s (up to those built at Darlington) seem to have been built with smooth-sided water tanks slung under the locomotive, whereas later ones adopted ribbed tanks.*
Ian James (D1462)

Above: *A further give-away to the former gangway doors on this batch of modified locomotives was the small lip at the base of where the doors had previously been. The later-built central headcode locomotives were free of this feature and they also carried a few extra handrails and different lamp iron positions, although 40060 at least has acquired most of these when seen on page 45, 40064 (D264) is seen here without the extras. When seen close-up from this angle their solid appearance was clear, as in this view of 40064 awaiting the chance to move south again from Inverness on 3rd September 1978.*

Officially they should not have been seen north of Inverness, but we have seen evidence of at least one making it as far as Bonar Bridge in the late 1960s. None were allocated to the Highland capital, but their appearance there was quite commonplace at one time. Although 40064 was a long-time Haymarket locomotive (which eventually transferred south), its classmates 40066, 40161 and 40165 worked their whole lives allocated to Haymarket with a combined service record of 60 years to the Depot. Crewe Works scrapped 40064 after withdrawal in 1982. Colin Whitbread (D1463)

Below: *When 40065 was seen in London on 8th May 1980 prior to working the 14.15 Kings Cross - Edinburgh Waverley service, it had been modified with some gentle curves around the headcode boxes in the fashion of the later-built locomotives and a sealed up nose. However, with an unmodified locomotive, the nose would have been tiresome for the crew, even if it was a warm summer day as an endless draught came through from the access doors. This must have been noted very quickly on the duties expected of Haymarket locomotives, so modifications were made to weld up the nose doors. Similar treatments were also found on the access doors of the Class 24, 25, 26 and 27 locomotives that were based there. This was both very sensible and commendable and it was to prove a practice that spread elsewhere, including south of the border, as time progressed. Some appear to have been dealt with during works visits, while others came at practical necessity following minor collisions and some may have been tackled at Depots from time to time.*

Colin Whitbread *(D1464)*

Above: *In examining the ongoing legacy of the original idea for easy access between locomotives we now see the former Healey Mills locomotive 40100 baring all on an Open Day at Swindon Works on 6th June 1981. Although much has been said about the front doors, surely the top doors cannot have been draught resistant when rattling along at speed? During this period much component recovery work was carried on at the Works although just how much of what was removed would actually be used is another matter. This locomotive was delivered as D300 to Crewe North (5A), but like so many of the Class it appears to have been sent there for acceptance from the nearby Works. The ER examples all took up their first shed allocations straightaway. Rather than being allocated to Doncaster (36A), the reality was that they were first gathered at Doncaster Works, who then sent them on to the depots once they were satisfied with their new locomotives. Withdrawn at the end of October 1980, 40100 remained at Swindon until fully broken up by the end of June 1981. The programme to refurbish the 4-CEP and 4-BEP slam-door electric stock for the Southern Region was also in full swing at this time, as can be seen from the stock in the background.*
Adrian Healey/Steve Ireland Collection (D1465)

Below: *Retaining its discs and showing an express working, 40095 at St. Helens Junction on 23rd February 1979 whilst in charge of an Aintree-Southampton Freightliner service. The modification of welding up the doors began in the late 1960s on LMR based locomotives, with several noted as still retaining their 'D' prefix in green livery. Some of these would be treated at one end only (often as a result of light collision damage), others at both ends! This modification was not just confined to the disc headcode variety as split-headcode machines also either had their doors welded up or plated over. The town of St Helens (close to Rainhill) was once a much busier location for the railway and was situated in an industrial landscape that has changed greatly today. A visitor here in earlier days would have been able to take in several locomotive sheds in a day within this area. Many of the names of these sheds, such as Plodder Lane, will be unknown to the majority of our readers who missed out on the steam era.*
Leonard Ball (D1466)

Above: *Many railway enthusiasts will have visited Scarborough at one time or another, either to experience a day out to the coast before scheduled steam services ended in 1967, or in more recent times to record the many steam specials that have been run from York to Scarborough using preserved locomotives. Some of these travellers would also have been aware of the Class 40s on the route and even enjoyed seeing them, while others will have even travelled on a scheduled Class 40 service or on one of the Merrymaker services that ran into the resort town behind these particular locomotives. For diesel enthusiasts the heyday of 'heritage traction' (as we now tend to call it) could best be enjoyed when Class 40s were being used, as we see here when 40139 pulls away from Scarborough with the 13.00 service to Manchester on Saturday 25th July 1981. Formerly D339, this 1961-built locomotive was withdrawn in 1982. Colin Whitbread (D1467)*

Top Right: *Journeys by diesel haulage have proved every bit as popular as steam specials, as the enthusiasts who have packed out 40044 on 12th January 1985 would be able to testify. Despite the snow seen during this stop at Derby, nothing will spoil their journey behind the former D244 as it heads towards York during its last days. Along with 40012 on the Birmingham - York service, 40044 is thought to have been the last Class 40 to work a scheduled BR service!*
Steve Ireland Collection (D1468)

Bottom Right: *Another working toward the end of Class 40 operation saw 40086 (D286) engaged on freight duties at Warrington on 27th July 1984. Although it has retained its headcode discs, it cane be seen that the nose door has been welded shut at one end.*
Steven Feltham (D1469)

Top Left: *The end of the Class 40s, as far as scheduled passenger trains went came after the 16.08 Birmingham-York service on Sunday 27th January 1985 behind 40012. Apart from D200/40122, the final Class 40 was departmental locomotive 97405, which was withdrawn in March 1987. By the end, the cabs of these engines were well worn, as shown by the extensive use of insulating tape inside the cab of 40051 which is captured whilst on railtour duty at Paddington on Sunday 9th October 1977. For would-be drivers of a Class 40 the cab details provide a tempting image, but there is not sufficient room in this book to describe their functions in detail.The former D251 was broken up at Doncaster Works in 1978.*
Colin Whitbread (D1470)

Bottom Left: *This photograph of 40075 (D275) was taken after the locomotive was condemned in July 1983. After being stored at Thornaby Depot on Teesside for four months when withdrawn in early 1982, it went to Derby Works. It then lingered for several years before it was moved on to Vic Berry's premises at Leicester to become one of only six Class 40s to be broken up there, the others being 40046, 40060 (as 97405), 40063, 40132 and 40163. The ignominious end finally came for 40075 in February 1987. Note the remains of the York (YK) depot sticker and the data panel, whilst above the number an enthusiast has chalked a final farewell message.*
Steve Ireland Collection (D1471)

Top Right: *The original style of nameplates applied to English Electric Type 4s carried a representation of a ship's wheel and the colours of the appropriate shipping line on a pennant in the centre, and a similar style of nameplate was fitted to D306/40106. This was named* **Atlantic Conveyor** *on 11th August 1984 after the Cunard ship that was lost in the Falklands campaign of 1982, and to recognise the valuable contribution of the men and women in the Merchant Navy during times of conflict. The set fitted to D210 on 12th May 1960 was (it seems) in place until sometime in 1971.*
Steve Ireland Collection (D1472)

Centre Right: *Not a great deal of information has been published on the unofficial names or indeed the painted nameplates on those Class 40s that originally carried a cast nameplate during the 1960s and early 1970s. This example painted onto 97405 (40060) is much more eloquent than the crudely-stencilled names of the likes of* **Dracula** *seen on 40129, which was not carried for very long and in the style of 40137* **Trojan**, *seen earlier on page 39. Other names unofficially applied to Class 40s included 40104* **Warrior**, *40131* **Spartan**, *40132* **Hurricane**, *40134* **Andromeda**, *40145* **Panther**, *and 40164* **Lismore**.
Steve Ireland Collection (D1473)

Bottom Right: *Here we have a good example of how the sides of the Class 40s were often treated after their nameplates had been removed; especially when the bolts were reversed and fitted with nuts to block up the holes. Another thing to bear in mind about the former nameplate fixings, as seen here on 40012* **Aureol**, *was the fact that the nameplates were not solid and were simply hollowed-out behind. However they had a webbing ridge inside this hollow to sustain these fixings as you might see if you are fortunate enough to see one. As far as is known, just one nameplate from the class is on public display, that being off D222* **Laconia**, *which is on display at the National Railway Museum in York. However, whilst replicas can be seen on the two preserved named Class 40s, 40012* **Aureol** *and 40013* **Andania**. *These look considerably better than the painted version shown here on 40012.*
Steve Ireland Collection (D1474)

Above: *A sylvan setting under the trees on a crisp day at BREL Crewe Works allows us to recall the scene copied at Swindon and Doncaster Works, as lines of redundant Class 40s await their time with the cutters. This selection on the 16th February 1985 includes 40181, 40195, 40143 and 40004. While many views show the condemned as very faded specimens after many months out in the sun, this collection looks as though they could be returned to service once again very quickly if required. However with so many Class 56s and 58s, and the (albeit late) arrival of Class 60s, there would be little freight work for them to handle. The chance of seeing six or more Class 40 'Whistlers' during a short spell at places like Blackpool, Chester or Manchester Victoria on holidaymaker trains was finally over.* Steve Ireland Collection (D1475)

We hope that you have enjoyed this look back at the Class 40s. May we also offer a reminder that all of these published shots are available to purchase as duplicate slide copies direct from Strathwood.

Send £5.00 for an extensive catalogue listing of these and many thousands of other shots available in colour, complete with sample slide.

Or visit the websites:
www.strathwood.com or www.railwayslide.co.uk